MW01231542

The New Civility

By Sol Chaneles:

Losing in Place (1972)
The Open Prison (1973)

By Sol Chaneles and Jerome Snyder:

"that pestilent cosmetic, rhetoric" (1972)

The New Civility

by

Sol Chaneles

illustrations by

Claudie Chaneles Grandberg

and others

Grossman Publishers   *New York*   *1973*

To Kathy
and Ira

Contents

Introduction

LADIES AND GENTLEMEN:

A society sworn to justice cannot tolerate distinctions among people other than those that Nature, in its genial and mysterious way, has imposed as a precondition for all life.

Where there are rulers and ruled, where there are coercers and coerced, there can be no justice. A society suffers a loss of momentum toward justice when people are arbitrarily assigned to social ranks and given or denied advantages according to these ranks, or when the outmoded trappings of elitism are confused with decency, consideration, and cultivation.

All societies, at present, are weighted down by rules, customs, and lethal weaponry sanctified by laws that set one group against another, cause humiliation to one for the benefit of another, provide the powerful ingredients of survival to some at the expense of others. Social distinction based on snobbism, tradition, protocol, or corporate regulations are patently unjust restraints on freedom. The very best that can be said about them is that they are pathetically comic. In 1972, for example, at a civic convocation in France, invited guests were permitted to enter the reception hall, to be seated, to speak, and so forth in accordance with a hierarchy of thirty-six ranks. The last to be seated and fed were:

30. auctioneers
31. doormen and ushers in public buildings
32. salesmen of marine insurance
33. lower-echelon civil servants employed by the administrative unit known as the prefecture

34. Lower-echelon civil servants employed by the municipality or township
35. employees of charitable organizations
36. firemen

Distinctions and privileges of rank originating from times of the royal courts are faithfully preserved in Great Britain—that bastion of democracy clinging tenaciously to the last vestiges of symbolic monarchy. The hierarchical lists are longer than those in France, and some of the impoverished dignitaries, near the bottom, often must rent appropriate garb to convey the outward appearances of nobility. It is the same in those societies pledged to the abolition of classes, like the Soviet Union and the People's Republic of China, though the lists of rank are somewhat shorter. And the dreary sameness persists in the United States, where the avowal of justice has been louder, has lasted longer than in all the others combined.

Justice is not to be found in the courts of law. Those places proliferate in lawyers, judges, laws, Latinisms, legalistic acrobatics, and the triumph of the status quo and the powerful, who are its advocates against the weak yearning for change.

Justice can only be found in oneself and in the relations of one toward another. It is a living, vital thing only to the extent that people believe and act upon its promptings.

> I believe because not to believe is to become as lead, to be prone and rigid, forever inert, and to waste away.
>
> *Henry Miller*

To believe is a private matter. Acting upon the impulses of justice, to act justly, is the subject matter of civility.

> It is part of the highest civility if, while never erring yourself, you ignore the errors of others.
>
> *Erasmus*

To be just implies the expectation of justice at the

hands of others; civility is a desire to receive it in turn.

The civility of America began by continuing the outward forms and appearances of her royal colonizers, England, France, Spain. To that base was added, through discrete borrowing, slavish imitation, and downright aping, the manners and mannerisms of the European courts as these evolved through revolution, war, industrialization, urbanization, and the claims of the bourgeoisie that they too, through money, sumptuous residences, gilt carriages, and silk stockings, were entitled to the perquisites of social rank, entitled to be treated with special esteem, entitled because of their bank accounts to be considered well-bred.

The old civility required little more than costly possessions, genteel birth, and good manners. The old civility expected considerable deference to social rank—that rank hierarchy of possession and privilege—but gave pitifully little. Esteemed for their courtly good manners, George Washington and Benjamin Franklin summed up civility in brief homilies. Said the former:

> Sleep not when others speak, sit not when others stand, speak not when you should hold your peace, walk not when others stop.
>
> *George Washington, 1748*

His ambassador to the ballrooms of the French Court, in a quintessential paean to elitism, said:

> Be civil to all; sociable to many; familiar with few.
>
> *Benjamin Franklin, 1756*

Justice? In all their outpourings over long and prolific lifetimes, there is scarcely a mention.

The New Civility is justice in action.
The New Civility is belief in and consciousness of justice and the determination to be just.
So that civility is not confused with the clever ap-

peals of commercial propaganda that wound people's sensibilities so that they will buy a merchant's ware to salve the wound, there are some things, it should be emphasized, that civility is *not* concerned with:

> • the cut of your trousers, the length of your skirt, for neither nudity nor raiment have helped to bring peace to a troubled world or comforted the aggrieved
> • the alternation of men and women at the dinner table, for seating arrangements cannot remedy an overcooked roast or assuage the hunger for companionship
> • the felicity of utterance and grammar, for neither helped to abolish child labor, and neither contribute to the liberation of the millions suffering colonial oppression.

On the other hand, civility *is* concerned with:

> • a man yielding a seat to a woman, for she alone carries the seed of future generations
> • courtesy, for it permits people to approach each other as equals
> • manners, for they are the ways people may act upon impulses of justice

Civility is more than manners, more than courtesy, more than rules for behaving justly, and more than those things it chooses to ignore. In part, it is a state of mind; in greater part, it is the quality of behaving that leads directly to assuring others a fair share of the possessions, rights, and burdens that grow out of our common experience on a little planet.

> Manners are more important than laws. Upon them in a great measure the laws depend. The law touches us here and there, and now and then. Manners are what vex or soothe, corrupt or purify, exalt or debase, barbarize or refine us by a constant, steady, uniform, insensible operation, like that of the air we breathe in. They give their whole form and color to our

lives. According to their quality, they aid morals, they support them, or they totally destroy them.

Edmund Burke

The New Civility is not meant to preserve empty archaisms like writing "Dear So-and-So" to someone who is not endeared and may even be consummately and callously unresponsive to an individual's woes; it is not really important whether one wears fine leather boots or shredded gaiters when going on a hunt, for the innocent fox, hawk, buck, partridge, and rabbit are wholly apathetic to fads in costume.

The New Civility is spatial, architectural. It assures an arrangement of the environment so that the individual may be alone, so that there may be easy access to the many. Where there are obstacles in the environment based on rank, there can be neither communication nor justice. Where there are such obstacles, there is only warfare. Civility in war is the sublime absurdity; it calls to mind the deferential patience of the executioner as Charles I bade him wait a moment so that the king could move his beard aside on the chopping block, saying: "This beard of mine has committed no treason."

Good manners is the art of making those people easy with whom we converse. Whoever makes the fewest people uneasy is the best bred in the company.

Jonathan Swift, 1720

Civility is not bellicosity but combativeness. It calls for assertion, muckraking, blowing the whistle on sham, incompetence, and the inevitably sinister machinations of the politician, his masters, and his toadies.

Civility is not servility, the monotonous repetition of dull exercises according to some antique rule; rather, it is boldness in making the sun of justice shine more brilliantly. Where there is civility, there self-expression may flower without fear or timidity but with robustness.

What is the New Civility? It is

a taste for truth and beauty, tolerance, intellectual honesty, fastidiousness, a sense of humor, good manners, curiosity, a dislike of vulgarity, brutality and over-emphasis, freedom from superstition and prudery, a fearless acceptance of the good things of life, a desire for complete self-expression and for a liberal education, a contempt for utilitarianism and philistinism, in two words:—sweetness and light.

Clive Bell

Civility is the eschewal of all titles: sir, ma'am, Mr., Miss, Mrs., Ms., Your Highness, Monsignor, Judge, Doctor, Professor, Admiral, boss, and all the others. Titles represent rank—privilege, prerogative, advantage—instead of people.

Civility is not foppish snickering at the inadvertent slip of the tongue or the ambiguous construction resulting from some preoccupation. The mannered snobs of the Edwardian period regaled and instructed themselves with the following encounter:

Widow X: I'm so sorry you couldn't attend my husband's funeral.

Mr. Y: I'm sorry I was out of town; I would have enjoyed immensely being there.

But civility is the outspoken criticism and hearty laughter from the bowels of frustration directed against the masters of casuistry, deception, cruelty, contempt, and dissembling. It is an act of supreme civility to catcall and hoot down a dissimulating public official whose only recourse is to upbraid what he considers to be the hooting and catcalling of his detractors. Protest in the name of justice is gallantry. In an era of gigantic concentrations of power, the hoarding up of privilege and advantage, protest is the mark of the gentleman and gentlewoman. But there is more:

• The New Civility insists that a hand should not be laid upon a child in anger, not because the blow represents an excess of vanity, rather that a child should not learn injustice thereby.

• The New Civility insists that such simple virtues as kindness, openness, politeness, and consideration should be acted out wholeheartedly as signs of equality rather than as disguises for cunning oppression.

• The New Civility insists that one does not have to wear rent garments, hang gunny-sack curtains on the windows, or eat uncooked oats to prove a spiritual identity with the victims of injustice.

Civility is an exchange of glances, what is said when *i*'s are not dotted, *t*'s not crossed; it is a love song without music or words and to no one in particular.

The qualities of a gentleman and gentlewoman—honesty, generosity, bravery, wisdom, gracefulness, restraint, tenderness, valor, intelligence—are, without civility, pleasant ways to pick pockets, destroy, intimidate, suppress, and kill. With civility they are—alone and together—ways to share, to dignify, to celebrate the fragile flame of life, and to bring justice.

At least five generations have gone into the making of this book. Five generations—not in the usual sense of family trees or prettified recollections or faded photographs, but five generations of real, live people. Some have left the scene of their wanderings, others are vibrantly in our midst; none were capable of moralizing, sermonizing, causing, deliberately or inadvertently, the slightest injury to anyone; all lived and continue to live by the New Civility that this book attempts to make coherent.

Some lived in thatched huts with packed earth as flooring, and labored in order that they might rest and study; others dwelt in castles, finding merriment in wild sleigh rides through snow-filled forests, howling wolves following in pursuit; others were witnesses to five wars in as many generations; others awoke before sunrise to stand in line under freezing rain to fetch a free bottle of milk for starving children; others picked leaves; others had their heads smashed on picket lines by paid thugs. One of them was blind but could not allow herself to appear in the presence of others unless the colors of her apparel were in complete harmony; another tried to stretch the day beyond its limits in order to give comfort to the aggrieved; and another succeeded in stretching the day in order to give skills to untutored hands so that they might live with undreamed-of dignity. The fifth generation has scarcely come to know the unfathomable nobility of people and the untold beauty of the world.

We cling to them as we cling to the future and this very moment. If civility could be expressed in a single thought, it would be a way of saying to all people, in the words of Goethe, "O stay, thou art so fair."

The New Civility

Admiration

Things not understood are admir'd.

Thomas Fuller, 1732

The greatest admiration gives rise not to words but to silence.

Musonius, A.D. 65

Often, those who seek admiration are really reaching out for approval. If approval is deserved, it should be given easily, openly, conveying a sense, at the same time, that it is fit to do so.

Advice

Old men delight in giving good advice as a consolation for the fact that they can no longer set
bad examples.

La Rochefoucauld

Advice is judged by results and not by intentions.

Cicero, 49 B.C.

'Tis easier to advise the suffering than to bear suffering.

Euripides, 438 B.C.

Who so loveth correction loveth knowledge:
But he that hateth reproof is brutish.

Book of Proverbs

Advice can no more be withheld than can breathing. We advise by example, by preventing someone's misfortune, by giving approbation, or by a display of scorn so timed and delivered that it is instructional rather than disgusting. Shun advice from those counselors who are inclined to answer with fortune-cookie parables and proverbs. Avoid counselors who cannot or will not back up their advice with deed or cash. To seek and give advice are ways of entwining your life with another's, and civility exacts involvement.

Alcohol

The vine bears three kinds of grapes: the first
of pleasure, the next of intoxication, the third
of disgust.

Anacharsis, 590 B.C.

Thomas Jefferson (1743–1826), author of the
Declaration of Independence and the Statute for Reli-
gious Liberty in Virginia and founder of the University
of Virginia, began, at age sixteen, to study law—a field
of endeavor dominated at that time by two ideals: virtue
and civility. Few people whose lives exemplified those
ideals have graced the American experience so richly.
From the time he reached his majority until old age there
were two things that Jefferson did each day without fail:
he drank a glass of wine at dinner and he soaked his feet
in a bucket of hot water before retiring. He soaked his

feet when he was alone and drank that single glass of wine whether with company or alone. One, both, either, or neither of these habits may have shaped the concepts and practices of justice and liberty in America and wherever the ideas and words of Jefferson have flowered.

Appearance

Be ever decorous when you enter and when you leave.

Talmud

At least in part because of our own negligence and permissiveness, we find ourselves living in what I am compelled to label the Age of the Slob—a time when slovenliness in personal hygiene, appearance, speech, and habits, immorality and obscenity publicly flaunted, a slothful, disinterested shoddiness in the performance of one's tasks, and a monumental self-centeredness which manifests itself not merely in discourtesy but in a churlish disregard of the rights of others and the niceties of human relationships in a truly civilized society —all seem to be the order of the day.

Theodore M. Black, 1972

Appearances deceive most frequently because the message isn't clearly stated; the message is often blurred because its purpose is fuzzy. A "good" appearance is one that is distinguished by forthrightness and clarity; it is a precondition for discourse.

Appreciation

He that makes himself an ass must not take it
ill if men ride him.

The Farmer's Almanac, 1795

Next to ingratitude, the most painful thing to
bear is gratitude.

Henry Ward Beecher

You pray in your distress and in your need;
would that you might pray also in the fullness
of your joy and in your days of abundance.

Khalil Gibran

Show it! Show it often and in as many ways as
the mood strikes you, but never in proportion to the vol-
ume, difficulty, cost, or whatever of what it is that com-
mands your respect and attention. A nod is often better
than a spoken "thank you," a touch of the hand better
than a gilded greeting card, a smile better than a formu-
larized note.

Assertiveness

The partisan, when he is engaged in a dispute, cares nothing about the rights of the question, but is anxious only to convince his hearers of his own assertions.

Socrates

The faculty of doubting is rare among men. A few choice spirits carry the germs of it in them, but these do not develop without training.

Anatole France

Too much doubt is better than too much credulity.

Robert G. Ingersoll

The majority of mankind is lazy-minded, incurious, absorbed in vanities, and tepid in emotion, and is therefore incapable of either much doubt or much faith.

T. S. Eliot

The vultures of insincerity plunge down, destroy, and feed on the innocent carcass of equivocation. No assertion spoken with understanding of the matter can be reproached. There is no such thing as a foolish question—only uninformed, hence foolish, answers. Assert, assert, assert!

Avoidance

I like long walks, especially when they are taken by people who annoy me.

Fred Allen

Do nothing in great haste, except catching fleas and running from a mad dog.

The Farmer's Almanac, *1811*

If, of all sad words of tongue or pen,
The saddest are "It might have been,"
More sad are these we daily see,
"It is, but it hadn't ought to be."

Bret Harte

Little things affect little minds.

Benjamin Disraeli

Look for, unravel, accept and reflect on contradictions in order to recognize and avoid them in the future. To know what a thing is not is part of knowing what it is. Avoid nuisances, but without showing annoyance. Often what is irksome isn't fully understood; when it is, it should be courted with pleasure.

Bluntness

Love of candor without the will to learn casts
the shadow called rudeness.

Confucius, 500 B.C.

Speaking, asserting, doing—all anticipate a re-
sponse. Bluntness should be gauged to facilitate a re-
sponse and not to thwart it.

Body

She whose body's young and cool
Has no need of dancing-school.

Dorothy Parker

I am fearfully and wonderfully made.

Psalms 139:14

As the great mysteries of the human body are revealed by advances in biology, chemistry, and biophysics, people will be more confident of all the genial things the body is capable of achieving with a little understanding and care. Body ignorance, body fear have led to the creation of giant industries that exploit and capitalize on these fears. There are deodorants and perfumes that use noxious, often poisonous, snythetic aromatic hydrocarbons; worthless food supplements; and ineffective analgesics. There are shoes that deform the feet, instruments that deform the bosom, needles that pierce the ears, fraudulent pomades for growing hair or making it disappear, and spurious ideas and prejudices that deform the spirit and mind. Understand your body and allow it to enjoy the right of speaking with as much freedom and restraint as you would with words.

Ceremony

It is superstitious to place one's hopes in ceremonies; but it is arrogant to refuse to submit to
them.

Blaise Pascal

Every country, every city, every profession has
its own particular form of civility. In my child-
hood I was painstakingly disciplined in ceremonial forms so as not to ignore them and to
exercise them properly. I love ceremony, but I
am not so blindly submissive to it that my
freedom is diminished thereby. Ceremony has
a number of forms that are plainly bothersome
—these are better forgotten by discretion
rather than by error, and one is not, as a con-
sequence, made less gentlemanly. I have often
seen men made uncivil by an excess of civility,
irksome from courtesy.

Montaigne

Therefore I hold this for certain: that in each
one of us there is some seed of folly which, once
it is stirred, can grow indefinitely. So I suggest
that our game this evening should be to discuss
this subject and that each one of us should
answer this question: "If I had to be openly
mad, what kind of folly would I be thought
likely to display?"

Baldassare Castiglione

Ceremonies celebrate the human spirit. They should be pursued with ardor. When most solemn, they teach and inspire about our common lot, how to be brave at the abyss, to relieve the momentary anguish of others, to believe that no one, except by choice, can be wholly alone. When most lighthearted, they prove that laughter is among the very few differences between mankind and the lower animals.

Ceremony is tedious and bothersome when the participants have no voice in determining its form and substance; it is odious when it imposes form without substance. Ceremonies that deride the human spirit should be assiduously eschewed: military parades and all their mindless imitators, including martial music and drum majorettes; initiations in fraternal or sororal societies requiring acts of submission, self-mutilation, and humiliation; testimonials for those whose deeds deserve a noose rather than praise; and all ceremonies that mark an end instead of a beginning. Ceremonies that rejoice in the solidarity of the human species should not be avoided simply because there will be tears, raucous laughter, ethnic jokes, a wearisome litany of platitude, the mawkish sentimentality of those who cannot act otherwise, or because one believes that it usurps time from other endeavors. It is civil to take part in ceremony, and the most important element of appropriate garb is one's humanity worn on the sleeve.

Clothing

That suit is best that best suits me.

John Clark, 1639

Costly thy habit as thy purse can buy,
But not express'd in fancy; rich, not gaudy,
For the apparel oft proclaims the man.

William Shakespeare

If anyone gives too great power to anything, too
large a sail to a vessel, too much food to the
body, too much authority to the mind, and does
not observe the mean, everything is over-
thrown, and in the wantonness of excess runs
in the one case to disorders, and in the other
to injustice, which is the child of excess.

Plato

Clothing is a private statement communicated
to the world. Its expression should be no more limited by
what's in your purse than speech, art, or literature. The
rule for clothing—made, borrowed, or bought—is iden-
tical with that for speech: appropriateness! Clothing can
often be too loud, but on some occasions voices have to
be raised to be heard. Understatement, like a whisper,
may represent either an excess of modesty or some subtle
purpose. Even tatters and garments begrimed, when calculated to speak, bestow and compel respect by sum-
mons to a common purpose.

Conversation

Conversation is an account of ourselves.

Ralph Waldo Emerson

The geniality of conversation consists much less in showing a great deal of it than in causing it to be discovered in others.

La Bruyère

Garrulity is irrelevant talking, or talking at length and without reflection. The garrulous man will sit beside someone whom he does not know and begin to praise his own wife, or tell the story of a dream he had the night before and then relate dish by dish what he had for dinner. As he warms to his business, he will remark that the younger generation have not the manners of the old, that the price of wheat has fallen, that there seem to be many foreigners in town, or that the ships will be able to put to sea after Dionysia. He will tell of what is being discussed in Parliament and even relate the speeches he himself was wont to make when a member of the assembly.

Theophrastus

Discourse intended for public consumption is entertainment whether it strikes the ear as trivia, demagogy, or wisdom, but it is not conversation. Conversation is essentially a private matter rarely permitting more than four or five to participate. While there are but few, very flexible, rules for public discourse, conversation is enhanced by ten commandments:

1. No interruptions!
2. No corrections!
3. No mumbling!
4. No haughtiness!
5. No expertise!
6. Clear thought!
7. Simple questions!
8. Brief replies!
9. Listen!
10. Share!

Correspondence

Drawn by
Alice Barber Stephens.

" 'I CANNOT HELP WHAT I SAY.' "

If there were a one-year moratorium on all forms
of written communication, thousands of acres of forests
would rise, but factories would shut; tens of thousands
of mail carriers would become unemployed; ships and

airlines receiving Government subsidies would experience economic trauma; and parents the world over would suffer great anxiety awaiting news from their offspring. The most vocal protests would come from manufacturers of junk mail.

Much correspondence has become mechanized, from engraved wedding invitations to printed "thank you" notes in reply to a printed bereavement card. A handwritten letter will serve any purpose, and the present availability of mechanical copying machines simplifies the task of keeping a copy of a letter if one is necessary. Obligatory notes can be avoided by the simple expedience of a brief telephone call. Unless you have a lot to say, letters should be short, legible, and to the point. A letter, like conversation, should express some quality of yourself in the language used and the form you choose in the shape and style of paper, the color of the ink, the design of the postage stamp. Some of the most delightful correspondence is received as a complete surprise. John Dewey, one of the world's most gracious philosophers, once said: "If you are deeply moved by some experience, write a letter to your grandmother. It will help you to better understand the experience and will give great pleasure to your grandmother."

Courage

Often the test of courage is not to die but to live.

Vittorio Alfieri, 1785

Perfect valor is to do, without a witness, all that
we could do before the whole world.

La Rochefoucauld

Courage scorns the death it cannot shun.

John Dryden, 1672

What seems to be impossible to accomplish is
a way of abandoning a method that doesn't work or a
method that takes much longer than expected. Doing
what is easy and natural, following one's bent, sometimes
takes more resolve—and effort—than scaling moun-
tains. Courage need not be flaunted; grant people the
qualities of perspective and alertness of eye to understand
for themselves the enormous effort you have put into
large and small things alike. It takes as much courage
to "make up" with a friend as to defy an unjust or illegal
command. Courage is rarely the sudden flame of defiance;
more often it is the minimal energy, day by day, year in
and year out, to resist as well as to extend a welcome to
those who have scorned. The best way to show it is by
trying to give it to others.

Courtesy

[The well-bred man] is neither a slave nor an enemy to pleasure, but approves or rejects as his reason shall direct. He is above stooping to flatter a knave, though in an exalted station;

nor ever overlooks merit, though he should find it in a cottage. His behavior is affable and respectful, yet not cringing or formal; and his manners easy and unaffected. He misses no opportunity wherein he can oblige his friends, yet does it in so delicate a manner that he seems rather to have received than conferred a favor. He does not profess a passion he never felt to impose upon the credulity of a silly woman; nor will he injure another's reputation to please her vanity. He cannot love where he does not esteem, nor ever suffers his passions to overcome his reason. In his friendship he is steady and sincere, and lives less for himself than his friends.

New York Weekly Magazine, *1796*

Etiquette can be at the same time a means of approaching people and of staying clear of them.
David Kiesman, 1950

Our youth of today love luxury. They have bad manners, contempt for authority, disrespect for older people. Children nowadays are tyrants. They contradict their parents, gobble their food, and tyrannize their teachers.

Socrates, 5 B.C.

Those early and distinctive American traits that were once perhaps quite properly associated with the American character—independence, manliness, inventiveness, egalitarianism, bootstrap ambitiousness, honesty—are now held up by the mass media, if at all, only in the most pallid and conventional terms and with a lack of interest that reveals how far we have come from the early American character.

John F. Day, 1962

Dissembling courtesy! How fine this tyrant
Can tickle where she wounds!

William Shakespeare

What courtesy waives, kindness bestows. It is an act neither of kindness nor of courtesy to give up what you never possessed; it is only pretense. If you do not know your rights or are not in command of them, being courteous or following a code of etiquette is an empty, ritual practice, a charade that masks apprehension. Those who know their rights and are secure in their exercise can and should share them without the least sense of deprivation. Our rights grow in proportion to their dissemination. People without rights cannot be expected to be courteous; courtesy should be vigorously pursued to right this wrong.

Courtship

Shacking up," trial marriages, communal living in pairs or hordes, living together as a form of protest against rigid conventions are good arrangements if they are entered into voluntarily and are open rather than secretive; they are bad if they try to prove some abstract point, are involuntary, or are so consummated as to conform with what others are doing. And what is true about contemporary experiments in domestic habitation is equally true about pursuing and wooing customs that are more familiar and have been the dominant style for only two hundred years or so and for only a relatively small portion of humankind. Neither the old forms nor the new can assure joyful memories worth remembrance; neither can assure that civilization will become more civil; neither will automatically lead to the intense loyalty and the ennobling bonds of friendship that characterize successful marriages; neither are relevant to bringing children into the world as an assertion of optimism or faith in the joyful outcome of life's hardy but predictable uncertainties. To experiment means that you are in full control of the ingredients and tools and environment of all that goes into an experiment.

Dancing

Get dancing!

The galaxy is not the exclusive province of astronomers and dreamers, it is the canopy of stars billowing over the dance hall of Creation.

Get dancing!

Decorum

The last temptation is the greatest treason:
To do the right deed for the wrong reason.

T. S. Eliot

Always do right. This will gratify some people
and astonish the rest.

Mark Twain

The good, as I conceive it, is happiness, happiness for each man after his own heart, and for each hour according to its inspiration.

George Santayana

To be useful, a tool, a mathematical equation, a gesture, a word, an explanation, or a glove must fit the circumstances that summon the ingenuity and desirability of each. A physician may have learned by rote all the bones of the body, but, lacking wit in making a fit between his knowledge and an occasion calling for it, he may leave a fracture badly set. To be decorous does not mean knowing rules or even applying them; rather decorum lies in doing what is appropriate toward each person and situation in accordance with a commitment to justice. This may call for breaking, improving, or inventing rules.

Deference

He who would honor learning and taste, and sentiment, and refinement of every sort ought to respect its possessors and, in all things but those which affect rights, defer to their superior advantages. This is the extent of deference that is due from him who is not a gentleman to him who is; this much is due.

James Fenimore Cooper, 1838

Outward things confer no quality other than taste (that can be cultivated), money (that can be accumulated), and self-expression (that can be communicated). Deference is necessary in order to train the eye to behold and to condition the ear to listen. One should defer to the wise so that learning can be more rapid and less painful and defer to the fool, for he too can teach, if only what to avoid. When young, one should defer to age, for older people are like lamps lighting the way into the great unexplored darkness; when old, one should defer to the young to steady their vision.

Dignity

Feel the dignity of a child. Do not feel superior to him, for you are not.

Robert Henri

No city ever becomes great by chance.

Seneca

To behave with dignity is nothing less than to allow others freely to be themselves, to delight in them within the framework of such a demanding guarantee. The dignity of others derives less from being themselves than from encouraging you to be yourself.

Discretion

Drawn by
Alice Barber Stephens.

When angry, count ten before you speak; if
very angry, an hundred.

Thomas Jefferson

One should not poke about into the mysteries of another's life. One should not impose one's moods, sentiments, or opinions uninvited on others. These twin rules apply only to private matters. There is no such thing as discretion when it concerns public matters; public things and public people permit neither mystery nor silence unless tyranny rules.

Drugs

Civility requires that when you are distressed in spirit or body you turn to the ministrations of friends or professional healers. Sometimes commiseration will result, but no ready cure. Some types of anguish, like some physical ills, can be remedied by time. Some can never be remedied. Others will often share the burdens of your distress, provided the path doesn't lead either to their destruction or to your own. It took thousands of years of experimentation to determine what kinds of drugs were beneficial for what kinds of ailments and the best circumstances for using them; no one has ever counted the tens of thousands or hundreds of thousands of those who died, became infirm, or suffered agonies beyond description while drugs were being crudely and unscientifically tested in the jungles, hamlets, and apothecary shops of ancient cities. Amateur, self-indulgent experimentation with drugs so as to test the capacities of unknown nooks and crannies of the brain is a sure way to destroy the basis for social life, for civility, and for life itself.

Education

I have two messages [for future generations]
—one on the intellectual side and the other on
the moral level. On the intellectual level: when

you study any matter ask yourself, "What are the facts?"

On the moral side: love is wise and hatred is foolish.

Bertrand Russell, 1960

The chief wonder of education is that it does not ruin everybody concerned in it, teachers and taught.

Henry Adams

We must believe the things we teach our children.

Woodrow Wilson

To listen is to learn—even if one listens by stealth. To speak is to teach—even when base gossip is spoken. Years of schooling do not add up to an education; years of self-instruction may not be equivalent to schooling or education. An illuminating insight may come suddenly or may evolve only after years of labor. Coming upon the right passage in the right book is often accidental; a lifetime can be spent in the pursuit of nonsense. Cultivation of a habit of attentive listening, knowledge about how to phrase an astute question so as to educe an informative reply, knowing when to speak and how to cloak in words the finest of what one understands, knowing where to look for understanding are all facets of education: these cannot be left to happenstance and should be pursued aggressively. At mealtimes or at social encounters one cannot offer a friend an empty dish.

Employees

The EMPLOYER AND the YOUNG MAN.

BY EDWARD W. BOK.

Throughout history the relations between employers and employees were based on the idea of a master-servant identity. Laws, traditions, job regulations back up the idea and make it palatable—for the employee, by obliging the employer to be benevolent; for the employer, by obliging the employee to be deferential. But all this is a vestige from the times when it was possible for employers to go about their profit-motivated tasks with no concern for the consequences of their business activities on people and the natural environment; employees were left with one alternative: take it or leave it.

The old civility for employees insisted on kowtowing, groveling, brownnosing, submissiveness, apple-polishing, and shining in the imagined sunshine of the boss's radiance. At best there was, or could be, polite indifference.

The New Civility for employees insists on deference and respect among equals; in the work environment as elsewhere all are equal. Higher pay and more leadership responsibility commensurate with more demonstrated ability anticipates more accountability to co-workers, a more rather than less active commitment to the rules that pertain to equals.

Entertaining

Inviting a Friend to Supper

Tonight, grave sir, both my poore house, and I
    Doe equally desire your companie:
Not that we thinke us worthy such a ghest,
    But that your worth will dignifie our feast,
With those that come; whose grace may make that
      seeme,
    Something, which, else, could hope for no
    esteeme.
It is the faire acceptance, Sir, creates
    The entertaynment perfect: not the cates.
Yet shall you have, to rectifie your palate,
    An olive, capers, or some better sallade
Ushring the mutton; with a short-leg'd hen,
    If we can get her, full of egs, and then,
Limons, and wine for sauce: to these, a coney
    Is not to be despair'd of, for our money;
And, though fowle, now, be scarce, yet there are
      clarkes,
    The skie not falling, thinke we may have larkes.
Ile tell you of more, and lye, so you will come:
    Of partrich, pheasant, wood-cock, of which some
May yet be there; and godwit, if we can:
    Knat, raile, and ruffe too. How so'ere, my man
Shall read a piece of VIRGIL, TACITUS,
    LIVIE, or of some better booke to us,
Of which wee'll speake our minds, amidst our
      meate;
    And Ile professe no verses to repeate:
To this, if ought appeare, which I not know of,
    That will the pastrie, not my paper, show of.

Digestive cheese, and fruit there sure will bee;
    But that, which most doth take my *Muse*, and
       mee,
Is a pure cup of rich *Canary*-wine,
    Which is the *Mermaids*, now, but shall be mine:
Of which had HORACE, OR ANACREON tasted,
    Their lives, as doe their lines, till now had lasted,
Tabacco, *Nectar*, or the *Thespian* spring,
    Are all but LUTHERS beere, to this I sing.
Of this we will sup free, but moderately,
    And we will have no *Pooly'*, or *Parrot* by;
Nor shall our cups make any guiltie men:
    But, at our parting, we will be, as when
We innocently met. No simple word,
    That shall be utter'd at our mirthfull boord,
Shall make us sad next morning: or affright
    The libertie, that wee'll enjoy to night.

                     Ben Jonson

Entertaining can be a collective, communal affair or one that is very individualistic and personal. Either way it can be elevating and memorable or disappointing and soon forgotten. Neither way is it indispensable for preserving friendship or family ties.

Entertaining that overly emphasizes food at the expense of care may result in a cheerless Lucullan orgy or digestive trauma, while care that gives insufficient attention to food is rather like Mother Hubbard sending engraved invitations to look upon her bare cupboard. Thus the vital element of entertaining is care, whether it. is preprandial (cocktails and snacks), prandial (breakfast, brunch, lunch, dinner), or postprandial (dessert, "tea" or "coffee," nightcap or a casual "drink"); whether it is at home, in a club, or in a public place; whether it responds to a special ceremonial occasion, like a wedding, a birthday, a promotion, a graduation, a holiday, or a memorial.

How an invitation to be entertained is extended is important—crucially important if the occasion is to fulfill all or most of the expectations of the host(s). A telephone invitation, a plain note, or an elaborately engraved invitation is important in proportion to the importance attached to the mood of the occasion. It is not imperative that a guest, man or woman, old or young, rise as another guest enters the room. This is often determined by the mood of the occasion itself, the size of the room, and the number of guests and their familiarity with one another.

How a person eats is as important as the care devoted to the preparation and serving of food. There is a genuine difference in the way food looks and tastes if it is served on paper plates rather than on pottery, porcelain, or golden platters. Beer, wine, water, apple cider, or whatever beverage, gain or lose if they are served in glasses instead of cups, in crystal instead of plastic.

Utensils, napkins, seating arrangements, the hour and date of entertaining are important only to the extent that they provide the host and hostess with additional ways of caring for their guests. Guests are expected to reciprocate this concern and care toward their host and hostess, toward their fellow guests, and toward themselves. When food is prepared with the use of certain utensils in mind, these should be used simply and attentively, not because it is bad to hold a knife in the left hand or cut salad with a spoon but because to do so violates the inherent drama of the entertainment, which has been planned with care. Seating arrangements at table reflect concern that neighbors should enjoy one another's presence. There are uncivil things that give offense to such concern, like making noises that disrupt conversation, like so placing one's elbows on the table that they block vision, like telling stories drawn from the annals of evil that distress some, embarrass others, and give offense to all.

Everything about entertaining should reflect infinite care—from the lights to the temperature of the food to what is said in greeting and parting and after the entertainment.

Etiquette

The true essentials of a feast are only fun and feed.

Oliver Wendell Holmes

The total want of all the usual courtesies of the table, the voracious rapidity with which the viands were seized and devoured, the strange uncouth phrases and pronunciation; the loathsome spitting, from the contamination of which it was absolutely impossible to protect our dresses; the frightful manner of feeding with their knives, till the whole blade seemed to enter into the mouth; and the still more frightful manner of cleaning the teeth afterwards with a pocket knife soon forced us to feel that we were not surrounded by generals, colonels, and majors of the old world; and that the dinner hour was to be anything rather than an hour of enjoyment.

Mrs. Frances Trollope, 1827

Comfort, opportunity, number, and size are not synonomous with civilization.

Abraham Flexner

If I am not worth the wooing, I surely am not worth the winning.

Henry Wadsworth Longfellow

To speak ill of others is a dishonest way of praising ourselves; let us be above such transparent egotism. . . . If you can't say good and encouraging things, say nothing. Nothing is often a good thing to say, and always a clever thing to say.

Will Durant

The tendencies of democracies are, in all things, to mediocrity, since the tastes, knowledge, and principles of the majority form the tribunal of appeal. This circumstance, while it certainly serves to elevate the average quali-

ties of a nation, renders the introduction of a
high standard difficult. Thus do we find in literature, the arts, architecture, and in all ac-
quired knowledge, a tendency in America to
gravitate towards the common center in this,
as in other things, lending a value and estima-
tion to mediocrity that are not elsewhere given.

James Fenimore Cooper

Treating the commonplace with the feeling of
the sublime gives to art its true power.

Except for politicians, the agents of inhumanity and
the sinister manipulators of injustice, the object of civility is to delight and ennoble all that vast brotherhood and
sisterhood who breathe the same air, drink the same
water, and walk the same earth. Let it be done, and done
quickly! Rely on whatever "rules" and guides are at hand,
but only as a starting point and never as ends in themselves. If you are not content with these rules and guides
as they are, laugh them away and ignore them. Make up
your own rules, provided they beat a path to mutual en-
richment and joy. Forms that cannot accomplish this
simple object should be rigorously abandoned. Life is al-
together too brief to squander even a fleeting moment on
trivia.

Food

Haëre maï ta maha. (Come and eat with us.)

Tahitian proverb

Devour not voraciously lest you become offensive.

Apocrypha

Better a dinner of herbs where love is, than a stalled ox and hatred therewith.

Book of Proverbs

The results of undernourishment and overnourishment are treatable illnesses. Excess, in one direction or the other, is often brought about by eating alone or in a disagreeable setting with people whom one doesn't know or among whom there is mutual hostility. Eating serves three purposes only: it is an occasion for sound nutrition, an occasion for delighting the senses, an occasion for civility. The ideal repast is one that combines the three.

Meals should be served and eaten at reasonable hours, in reasonable quantities, and in a setting that encourages amiable exchanges. Badly cooked food; or food that pretends, when, it fact, it has been drained of all pleasure and nutritive value by an excess of preparation; or food that is eaten in a setting requiring the observation of a plethora of outmoded, foolish rules are among the many avenues leading to indigestion. So are sneezing, yawning, nose-blowing, spitting, coughing, belching, picking teeth, and body-scratching during meals.

Friendship

The proper office of a friend is to side with you when you are in the wrong. Nearly anybody will side with you when you are in the right.

Mark Twain

Friendship is almost always the union of a part of one mind with a part of another; people are friends in spots.

Benjamin Disraeli

Choose thy friends like thy books, few but choice.

James Howell

Nearly all relationships, especially among blood relations, are marred by unilateral excesses: too much giving, often reluctantly accepted; or too much taking, often reluctantly given. Friendship is the exception: it cannot be replaced by vending machines that can merchandise most of the giving and taking of other kinds of relationships.

A friend bestows without expecting return or because something is due. Without bestowal—whether of heartbreak, the calumny of those who have been deceived, fatuity, glibness, the absurdity of adversity, the treasures of tenderness, or cold cash—there is no friendship.

A legacy is not an act of friendship although it may come torrentially and as a surprise, for it is only on the living that friendship may be bound. Only a friend may give unsolicited advice without giving offense, and only a friend may take one's time without trying one's patience. Even in taking, a friend bestows.

Gentleness

That he is gentil that doeth gentil dedis.

Chaucer

A soft edge to word and action honors the recipient and reflects neither weakness of purpose nor softheadedness.

Getting Oneself Together

All essential knowledge relates to existence, or only such knowledge as has an essential relationship to existence is essential knowledge.

Sören Kierkegaard

But self-examination, if it is thorough enough, is nearly always the first step toward change. I was to discover that no one who learns to know himself remains just what he was before.

Thomas Mann

Nothing requires a rarer intellectual heroism than willingness to see one's equation written out.

George Santayana

Being in command, at all times, of your feelings, your abilities, your appetite for life is indispensable if you are to grace the life of others with meaning and delight. Getting to that point requires that you gain personal "eyeball" experience, not to the point of surfeit but only so that you can readily distinguish between the genuine article and sham. This means traveling, doing, talking, reading, listening, testing, avoiding ruts or getting out of them, and feeling—knowing what the feelings mean and what the dazzling bounty of life offers for the way you choose to live. Self-knowledge that serves no purpose beyond oneself is a certain way to court stagnation and premature senility.

Gifts

Generosity is the flower of justice.

Nathaniel Hawthorne, 1850

The greatest grace of a gift, perhaps, is that it anticipates and admits of no return.

Henry Wadsworth Longfellow, 1871

The best part of a gift is the part of yourself that goes with it. Gifts given as an obligation are not really gifts at all: these are sacrificial things. Avoid obligatory giving as you would avoid sickness and taxes. Avoid also gifts of "white elephants"—those things that impose burdens instead of bestowing pleasure. Find as many occasions as you can for giving gifts—things that you make or purchase, always in proportion to what you can afford and to the pleasure you get in giving. Let no occasion prompt or expect gratitude, feigned or real delight, or, worst of all, reciprocation.

Gossip

It's mean, cruel, heartless, malevolent, unkind, evil, spiteful, harsh, vicious, inconsiderate, ungracious, malicious, brutal, and lacking in civility.

Don't!

Hair

Having a beard and wearing a shabby cloak
does not make philosophers.

Plutarch, A.D. 95

Thy beard is long, better it would thee fit
To have a shorter beard and longer wit.

Musarum Deliciae, seventeenth century

Give me a face
That makes simplicity a grace:
Robes loosely flowing, hair as free;
Such sweet neglect more taketh me
Than all the adulteries of art;
They strike mine eyes but not my heart.

Ben Jonson, 1609

Wear your hair the way you want with respect
to length, color, quantity, ornament, provided the wearing poses no risk to health, danger at work, or more care than you are able to give it without sacrificing other pursuits. Avoid that kind of rigid vanity that refuses to compromise a hairstyle in the name of friendship, affection, esteem, or harmonious relationships.

Heroes

When the imaginary saint or lover or hero
moves us most deeply, it is the moment when
he awakens within us for an instant our own
heroism, our own sanctity, our own desire.

William Butler Yeats

We shall continue to look up to people who
are decent and good because they have something to
share and qualities worth emulating. Slaves build
pedestals—they are commanded to—and the earth is
strewn with marble shards that were once bigger-than-
life statues of heroes. The newer heroes of our age are
deliberate creations designed and packaged to sell a
worthless pill or a worthless political agenda, or to pro-
mote progress by standing still. We fabricate, consume,
and discard heroes the way we do soap wrappings, and
soon we shall have no place to dispose of either. Let us
reject heroes once and for all—not because they per-
spire publicly, or drink to excess privately, or even because they shudder at the signs of their own frailties, but
rather because in accepting ourselves we can better see
the sun without obstruction. Ward off heroes by reaching
out to touch and share with those who are decent and
good.

Holidays

If all the year were playing holidays,
To sport would be as tedious as to work.

William Shakespeare

The holiest of all holidays are those
Kept by ourselves in silence and apart;
The secret anniversaries of the heart.

Henry Wadsworth Longfellow

Though the fool waits, the day does not.

French proverb

Every day should be passed as if it were our last.

Latin proverb

To be among people one loves, that's sufficient;
to dream, to speak to them, to be silent among
them, to think of them, to think of indifferent
things; but among them, everything is equal.

La Bruyère

Birthdays, baptisms, Christmas, Rosh Hashanah, marriages, anniversaries, July Fourth, Passover, All Saints' Day, Labor Day, and more, many more, should be avidly pursued as occasions for rest, festivity, rejoicing, gift-giving, sharing, dancing, singing, storytelling, and laughter, all with understanding that the central character, the central theme is life, humanity, our dependence one on the other, and the reaffirmation of the resolve that no one is free so long as there is someone in chains.

Every holiday, even the most solemn, should be the occasion for celebration and the demonstration of affection.

Home

Why don't you clean out the well? The air and the water of the farm must be kept pure, you know, cost what it will. A well ought to be cleaned out once a year, at least, if you want to have water that's fit to drink.

There's a waste in most of our drains that ought to be stopped. They are apt to taint the air, and bad air goes to swell up the doctor's bill. A "Dispensation of Providence" is more'n half the time nothing but foul air to breathe, and tainted water to go into the teapot. It's our own fault.

Let us take care of the pigpen, the cowyard, the sink drain, the outhouse, and stop the leaks in them all, if we want to live to three score and ten.

The Farmer's Almanac, *1881*

As much as I converse with sages and heroes, they have very little of my love and admiration. I long for rural and domestic scenes, for the warbling of birds and the prattling of my children.

John Adams, 1777

It is very difficult to understand anybody without visiting his home.

Gilbert Highet

The best security for civilization is the dwelling, and upon proper and becoming dwellings depends more than anything else the improvement of mankind. Such dwellings are the nursery of all domestic virtues, and without a becoming home the exercise of those virtues is impossible.

Benjamin Disraeli, 1874

Home is the ultimate proving ground for civility. It is where civilization flourishes—or ends. It is the definitive laboratory for social innovation. It is a place for renewal, never a haven or refuge. A house can be put on wheels and transported anywhere, but never a home.

A home cannot tolerate servants, domestics, "the girl," "the cleaning woman," the maid, "the kitchen mechanic," or "the help"—only working people who voluntarily enter into a contract providing decent wages, working conditions, and the civility of equals.

Home is not a way station: it is a profession of faith in life.

Home is not silverware, embroidered samplers, carpeting, color schemes, bric-a-brac, or furniture: it is where remembrances are harvested and the riddles of infancy and age answered by the unwavering light and intense warmth of tranquillity.

Honesty

No public man can be just a little crooked.

Herbert Hoover

Nobody can acquire honor by doing what is wrong.

Thomas Jefferson

Our minds possess by nature an insatiable desire to know the truth.

Cicero

All honor's wounds are self-inflicted.

Andrew Carnegie

Thou shalt not allow thyself to be mortified, to be exploited, to become the victim of anyone's whim or villainy, to be blinded by thine own vanity or the illusions of another, to brandish dissimulation as truth, to gull the gullible, to gain unfair advantage by thine own aura or seeming innocence, to dampen hope when it may still be or to hold it out where there is none.

Honor

Be glad at heart; but this wild joy restrain;
We may not rightly triumph o'er the slain.

Homer

Honor is, on its objective side, other people's
opinion of what we are worth; on its subjective
side, it is the respect we pay to this opinion.

Arthur Schopenhauer, 1851

The louder he talked of his honor, the faster
we counted our spoons.

Ralph Waldo Emerson

Politicians, military officers, and many business-
men are notorious collectors of laurel wreaths, plaques,
and medals. They lose no occasion to broadcast honors
bestowed on them, and there are but few occasions to
inform the public about how these honors have bought,
wheedled, and rigged. Beware honors! There is none in
killing someone or in making a killing. Academic, artistic,
and literary honors result from fierce competition and
Machiavellian machinations. Philanthropists get them as
an inducement to be philanthropic.

Avoid archaic incantations like "I have the honor
of announcing," "It is my honor to introduce," "It is an
honor to be here." Honor is the integrity of your feelings
and actions toward others, and, like breathing, it is a
vital sign that requires no special attention except when
it's not working properly.

Hospitality

Hospitality is a little fire, a little food, and an immense quiet.

Ralph Waldo Emerson

We often pardon those who bore us, but never those whom we bore.

La Rochefoucauld

Let thy foot be seldom in thy neighbor's house, lest he be weary of thee and hate thee.

Book of Proverbs

To visit someone's home, for an hour, an evening, a weekend, or longer, is one of the most sacred and joyous activities among civilized people. This is so for kin, friends, and acquaintances. Whether visiting or receiving, as guest or host, hospitality requires a single mutual obligation: discover and bring out what is best in each other. This can be done by offering or sharing an infinite number of things: conversation, thoughtful gifts, elaborate meals, perfumed soaps, exquisitely embroidered linens, flowers, an ever-present pot of coffee, or, simply, a glass of fresh water. The essence of hospitality is attentiveness among those sharing the visit. To divine and respond to a troubled heart in words or in silence, to listen without distraction, to do companionate things like listening to a record or looking at a television program or stamp collection or the new flooring in the kitchen, or to be enriched by the offering and acceptance of solitude are some of the hallmarks of hospitality. For many people, their own home, unhappily, is a torment because they are burdened by unsatisfied longings, because of wounds that only time can heal, or because they have not been able to accept the expression of themselves as it is reflected in their home. Thus, a so-called welcoming sentiment like "Make yourself at home" may either be pardonably trite or an outright offense. As guest or host, the setting and what is done with it and how food and beverage are prepared, arranged, and served are important only if they are the means to and not the object of hospitality. Use of one's home to further business or professional ambitions, under the guise of hospitality, transforms the sanctity of the hearth into the crass banality of the marketplace and should be avoided. Being host or guest out of obligation is unadulterated hypocrisy; obligation can be satisfied without trespass on the home or damage to mutual enlightenment that grows out of hospitality.

Hypocrisy

Woe unto you, scribes and Pharisees, hypocrites! for ye are like unto whited sepulchres, which indeed appear beautiful outward, but are within full of dead men's bones, and of all uncleanness.

Matt. 23:27

Three rules for avoiding hypocrisy:

• Get things done, but never promise them in advance.

• Reveal your mistakes, understand them, look in those places and to those people who can help to clarify the nature of the mistake; hiding a mistake makes slander of something that may have been innocent or inadvertent.

• Look for facts and their proof; speculate on ideas to your heart's content, but do not fabricate answers where there are none. To do otherwise is to wear the hypocritical mask of Cant, which is the principal disguise of politicians, government statisticians, hucksters, brigands, rogues, and demagogues.

Independence

He who waits to do a great deal of good at once will never do anything.

Samuel Johnson

Nothing is a greater impediment to being on good terms with others than being ill at ease with yourself.

Honoré de Balzac

I believe in individualism . . . up to the point where the individualist starts to operate at the expense of society.

Franklin Delano Roosevelt

I would rather sit on a pumpkin and have it all to myself than be crowded on a velvet cushion.

Henry David Thoreau

Whoso would be a man, must be a Nonconformist.

Ralph Waldo Emerson

Know what your rights are and exercise them to the fullest extent possible; know what the unfair burdens of others are so that you can lift them and share them as your own; brook no greater interference in your privacy than you would endure in your breathing; fend off the seductions of fanatics, and try to enlighten fools.

Jewelry

A well-wrought object is a pleasure to touch and to talk about. Since it delights, more men and women should adopt the practice of wearing it. The beauty of a thing is enhanced by its appropriateness for the person and for the occasion.

Justice

Poetic Justice, with her lifted scale;
Where in nice balance, truth with gold she
    weighs,
And solid pudding against empty praise.

Alexander Pope

Right knows no boundaries, and justice no
frontiers; the brotherhood of man is not a
domestic institution.

Judge Learned Hand

Seek neither license, where no laws compel,
Nor slavery beneath a tyrant's rod;
Where liberty and rule are balanced well
Success will follow as the gift of God
Though how he will direct it none can tell.

Aeschylus

There are over two million laws in the United
States, yet there is a constant cry "Justice! Justice! Where
is Justice?" More laws will not increase justice; more
lawyers will only bring more laws. Justice is not to be
found in the study of law but in the understanding of the
heart, hopes, and aspirations of mankind. Justice is the
most absolute of principles: sharing of rights, sharing of
burdens in accordance with each one's ability to exercise
the former and carry the latter. Civility is conduct in
conformity with these principles.

Language

Of all skill, part is infused by precept and part
is obtained by habit.

Samuel Johnson

It is a pity, indeed, to lack the ability of speaking well, or the good sense of keeping quiet.

La Bruyère

Language is a city to the building of which every human being brought a stone.

Ralph Waldo Emerson

Language is the expression of ideas, and if the people of one country cannot preserve an identity of ideas, they cannot retain an identity of language.

Noah Webster

The sole universal purpose of language is to facilitate precise understanding among people. Tears, shrieks, grumbling, grunting, and most gestures convey many different meanings at various places and times. Language enjoys immense privileges through endless variation and specialized purposes—the crude recording of a historical fact, proclamations that consecrate the human spirit or enlarge liberties, a clearly printed road sign at the right place, the invigorating or ennobling eloquence of words that have been well-sculpted by the tongue's wrist, persuasion, and justified vilification. There are many rules on how to fashion language with clarity and felicity to suit diverse purposes, and there are rules—conveniently flexible—about how words and phrases ought to look or sound when spoken or written, according to contemporary views. Rules change when understanding among people changes. Civility requires that bestowing, receiving, seeking understanding are preconditions for language. Misanthropes—the despisers of life and people—maintain a meaningless silence or are given to howling; they are bereft of language. Unjust people use language to masquerade corrupt and exploitative intentions—they seek to sow obfuscation, mistrust, and misunderstanding. Language, in its rhythms, sonorities, cadences, pauses, in its irresistible terseness or elaborately ornamental amplification, is the fittest universe of sound for civil people.

Loneliness

It is better to be alone than in ill company.

Stefano Guazzo

It is unpleasant to go alone, even to be drowned.

Russian proverb

Civility is not limited to how you conduct your-self toward others. Civility does not begin or end by treating oneself with the respect and cordiality gener-ously offered to others. Civility does not "begin at home," though it is tested there, nor is it a game calculated to thwart fears and pains of loneliness by compelling acts of false sociability. Because it is difficult to treat oneself to the grace bestowed on others, loneliness is difficult to avoid. Because it is painful you should always be pre-pared to respond to your own woes as you would to-ward another's agonies. Seek solitude, but avoid loneliness: in solitude you are never without the com-panionship of friends—past, present, and future; lone-liness is a vacuum.

Love

The rule that you are to love your neighbor becomes, in law, you must not injure your neighbor; and the lawyer's question, Who is my neighbor? receives a restricted reply. You must take reasonable care to avoid acts or omissions which you can reasonably foresee would be likely to injure your neighbor. Who, then, in law, is my neighbor? The answer seems to be persons who are so closely and directly affected by my act that I ought reasonably to have them in contemplation as being so affected when I am directing my mind to the acts or omissions which are called in question.

Lord Atkin, 1932

To understand oneself is the classic form of

consolation; to elude oneself is the romantic.

George Santayana, 1922

If you would be loved, love and be lovable.

Benjamin Franklin, 1755

There is no remedy for love but to love more.

Henry Thoreau, 1839

To love means to *admire*, to *appreciate*, to be *courteous*, to show *deference*, to endow with *honor*, to be *just;* all of these are treated in this book. To love also means other things, and these too are subject to the rules of civility.

Lying

Equivocation is half-way to lying, as lying the whole way to hell.

William Penn

A legend is a lie that has attained the dignity of age.

Blaise Pascal

I believe it is an established maxim in morals that he who makes an assertion without knowing whether it is true or false is guilty of falsehood, and the accidental truth of the assertion does not justify or excuse him.

Abraham Lincoln

When a hired killer knocks at your door inquiring for your friend, who is his intended victim, it is a perfectly justified lie to say that he is not at home. The United States Supreme Court has held that the taxpayer is justified in lying as much as he wants in order to keep from the state's ravenous maws as much as he can withhold. And the lawyer, doctor, and fisherman are given free vein to the lie for reasons above civility, above reason itself. We are spawning a multitude of authorities professing new techniques for lying and new justifications for the lie: alibis for failure to fulfill an agreed-on responsibility, muffled voice on the phone to thwart a creditor, breath sweeteners to disguise tippling, or a perfumed, illicit embrace. We have allowed the state and the giant corporations to create, at our expense, a vast apparatus to devise and disseminate lies—lies about atrocities, about injustice, about hunger and disease, about the shabbiness and danger of business practices and products. We have allowed ourselves to equivocate, to believe in the myth that our governmental and legal institutions are wedded to the ideals of impartial justice and to share thoughts with others that have the appearance but not the substance of fact.

There are three rules about lying:
- Lie to save a life, yours or someone else's.
- Speak in a straightforward fashion to child and adult alike about what you know and what you don't know, what is accepted on faith or as a matter of established fact.
- If ever in doubt, don't.

Marriage

Every man [in America] takes a wife as soon as he chooses, and that is generally very early;

no portion is required, none is expected; no marriage articles are drawn up among us, by skillful lawyers, to puzzle and lead posterity to the bar, or to satisfy the pride of the parties. We give nothing with our daughters; their education, their health, and the customary outset are all that the fathers of numerous families can afford. As the wife's fortune consists principally in her future economy, modesty, and skillful management, so the husband's is founded on his abilities to labor, on his health, and the knowledge of some trade or business.

Crèvecoeur, 1782

It is necessary to the happiness of man that he be mentally faithful to himself.

Thomas Paine

True friendship seeks three things above all others—the magnetic nobility of virtue, the delight of companionship, and the compulsion of need. We must accept our friend's criticisms, enjoy their company, and help them when called upon.

Isocrates

We should learn how to behave rightly to our own families and dependents, how to perfect our relations with our friends, and how to serve our country and our fellow-citizens.

Xenephon

A man and a woman agree to live under a common roof and through procreation or adoption to care for one or more children: when there is such agreement, there is marriage. Everything else said about things peripheral to the agreement is either circumlocutory cant or babel.

The agreement does not need—if the parties don't feel the need—certificates or ceremonies, but both are desirable since each celebrates in its own way an act of voluntary choice, free decision—the choice of life, the decision to perpetuate it for generations to come. Marriage is a celebration of life; certificates and ceremonies are ways of sharing morsels of the celebration with others.

Modesty

It is sometimes wise to forget who we are.

Publilius Syrus, 50 B.C.

Modesty antedates clothes and will be resumed when clothes are no more. Modesty died when clothes were born. Modesty died when false modesty was born.

Mark Twain

To speak about one's accomplishments that have been recognized by others as possessing some superior merits does not show a lack of modesty. It's purely factual and informative. To broadcast self-assessments of one's superior merits that have not been (or not yet been) recognized by others may be immodest and it also may be sheer self-deception. In a society where injustice thrives, that is, wherein one cannot effectively inform others about his legitimate needs and gain what is one's due, self-promotion is a perfectly acceptable form of self-expression and assertion. Frequently, sentiments about modesty are ways of encouraging someone to be silent in order to allow another to tell of his accomplishments. Practice modesty, but only when, based on facts alone, you are supremely confident of your accomplishments.

Money

Make all you can, save all you can, give all you can.

John Wesley

Money is like an arm or leg, use it or lose it.

Henry Ford

Money is not essential for the exercise of liberty or for satisfying the basic needs of humanity; it is only a conventional and convenient means toward those ends. It can neither provide enduring delight nor relieve genuine anguish. Bucks, like the ballot, do not guarantee either quality or intelligence; the importance and meaningfulness of the first two depend on the last two.

Opposition

Men are qualified for civil liberty in exact proportion to their disposition to put moral chains
upon their own appetites. . . . Society cannot
exist unless a controlling power upon will and
appetite be placed somewhere, and the less of it
there is within, the more there must be without.
It is ordained in the eternal constitution of
things that men of intemperate minds cannot
be free. Their passions forge their fetters.

Edmund Burke

Social reform is tantamount to wearing soft
bunting between the wrists and the chains. Radicalism
(from *radex*, meaning "the root") is a view toward oneself and others that rejects all that demeans the human
experience, all that oppresses man. Since evil cannot go
off on its own will, it must be opposed: resistance is
among the chief requirements of civility.

Pets

A nuisance when they tangle on the street.

• A distraction when receiving guests.
• Some people are allergic to them.
• When you want them to perform, they resist.
• It's best to keep them out of sight on those occasions when you want human rather than animal companionship.

Politics

None but the contemptible are apprehensive of contempt.

The Farmer's Almanac, 1835

We trust a man with making constitutions on less proof of competence than we should demand before we give him our shoe to patch.

James Russell Lowell

An honest politician is one who, when he is bought, will stay bought.

Simon Cameron, 1860

Nothing is politically right that violates civility. Politics and politicians are obstacles to civility. The chief enemy of civility is not bad taste but bad politics, bad politicians. So long as the visions of compassionate people are haunted by injustice, politicians must be viewed as its agent. So long as the rights and burdens of civilized life are shared unfairly, civility demands that the whistle of opprobrium be blown to identify those who profit from injustice—the politician and his patrons.

Praise

Great tranquility of heart is his who cares for neither praise nor blame.

Thomas a Kempis

Don't strew me with roses after I'm dead.
   When Death claims the light of my brow,
No flowers of life will cheer me: instead
   You may give me my roses now!

Thomas A. Healey

I can live for two months on a good compliment.

Mark Twain

Giving undeserved praise is more damaging than even the most intemperate but constructive criticism. Parents and friends are mere sycophants when, in the spirit of encouragement, they fawn on the accidental and casual playful acts of children instead of tactfully withholding approbation: they serve the cause neither of parenthood nor of friendship. When praise *is* deserved, heap it on as if there were no tomorrow: it is only an expression of gratitude for what you have received, a justifiable celebration of your own judgment and senses. When receiving praise, acknowledge it in the fewest possible words.

Prejudice

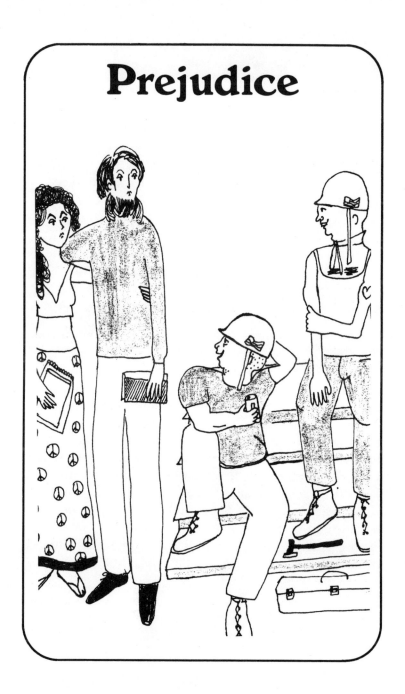

The prejudices of ignorance are more easily removed than the prejudices of interest; the first are all blindly adopted, the second willfully preferred.

George Bancroft

One may no more live in the world without picking up the moral prejudices of the world than one will be able to go to hell without perspiring.

H. L. Mencken

Honesty of thought and speech and written word is a jewel, and they who curb prejudice and seek honorably to know and speak the truth are the only builders of a better life.

John Galsworthy

The prejudgment of people and things is no more sinister than anticipation of the weather. No one will reprove you for avoiding foods you have never tasted, for staying out of waters you believe without proof to be dangerous, or for keeping at arm's distance ideas that you cannot or do not wish to make your own; yet castigations will inundate you if you harbor feelings or intuitions that someone is a rogue, a fool, or a hustler bereft of conscience. Live with your prejudices until they are proven right or wrong, but never, without the most convincing kind of proof, act to deny anyone his rights or access to them.

Pride

In reality, there is, perhaps, no one of our natural passions so hard to subdue as pride. Disguise it, struggle with it, beat it down, strike it, mortify it as much as one pleases, it is still alive, and will every now and then peep out and show itself. . . . Even if I could conceive that I had completely overcome it, I should probably be proud of my humility.

Benjamin Franklin

One man's ostentatious strut is another's self-effacing shuffle. Things have no power to speak for themselves until they have been shaped by purpose. The gift of oneself to a friend or lover implies feelings of pride—of worthiness—in oneself and toward the recipient. A home, children, pets, clothing, music, song, ideas are gifts, and pride in them does not enhance what they are: it only enhances the enjoyment of them. Pride is disruptive when it leads to an erroneous evaluation of what things really are.

Privacy

The right to be alone—the most comprehensive of rights, and the right most valued by civilized men.

Louis D. Brandeis, 1928

The guarantee of privacy when alone or in public places is a precondition for all civility. There are exceptions: the public official, the brigand, and the fool. Their actions cannot unfold without some measure of voluntary surrender of a portion of our privacy; thus, they must be held accountable, open to the widest, most intensive kind of public scrutiny. We inevitably lose privacy in proportion to our involvement with others and with cooperative or collective endeavors. An uneasy choice has to be made between the satisfactions of sociability and the blessing of absolute privacy. Though not easy, it is still a matter of choice. Where there is no choice, there is tyranny—the tyranny of intrusion and invasion and the death of civility, or the tyranny of hermitage.

Public Servants

Publicity is justly commended as a remedy for social and industrial diseases. Sunlight is said to be the best of disinfectants, electric light the most efficient policeman.

Louis D. Brandeis, 1914

Civil servants have raised incivility onto a pedestal. They are nowhere to be seen when they are needed; they have devised myriad and ingenious ways to justify their indifference and lethargy; they view the taxpayer who pays their wages not as a fellow citizen to be served but as an object of contempt, whose needs intrude on the sanctity of their insulated torpor. Civility requires that the slightest incivility of this multitude be brought to light, and, if they cannot be made to function at public expense, let them try to be self-supporting.

Public Speaking

There is no inspiration in evil and . . . no man ever made a great speech on a mean subject.

Eugene V. Debs

Speak clearly, if you speak at all;
Carve every word before you let it fall.

Oliver Wendell Holmes

A vessel is known by the sound, whether it be cracked or not; so men are proved by their speech, whether they be wise or foolish.

Demosthenes

If you are certain, let your certainty be known in every public place; if uncertain, all the more reason to let your uncertainty be known. Calculated silence can be a potent tool of persuasion, but indifference never can. A portion of each day should be given over to some public utterance.

Relations with Professional People

Professional people like nothing better than to hide their self-doubts, their fears, their limitations, and even their incompetence behind a mask of credentials, office trappings, and an unproven mystique of omniscience and skill. Magicians, necromancers, sorcerers, vampires, and alchemists, along with water diviners, are no longer among us in great numbers not because they failed to hold out hope but because they simply couldn't produce. Do not go blindly or innocently into the dentist's chair, onto the doctor's table, or beside the lawyer's desk without asking for complete understanding, a satisfactory sharing of what the professional knows and proposes and why. The eradication of doubt, to the extent that it is possible, is a precondition for equality in any relationship.

Rights

[A] function of free speech under our system is to invite dispute. It may indeed best serve its high purpose when it induces a condition of unrest, creates dissatisfaction with conditions as they are, or even stirs people to anger.

United States Supreme Court
Edwards v. South Carolina, 1963

The foolish and the dead alone never change their opinion.

James Russell Lowell

Only inalienable rights are governed by civility. Rights that accrue to position or are recognized because of an accumulation of wealth become the unfair burdens of others. Civility begins with the recognition of the rights of others, and it grows, by quantum leaps, as it assists others to the fullest enjoyment of rights.

Salutations

The most lucid and elegant manner of speaking is for naught when you have nothing to say. When greeting someone with whom you have had or wish to have pleasant associations, a minimal friendly nod will do. There is no maximum salutation except those dictated by time, location, and circumstances. A single kiss on the cheek between a man and a woman is salutation American-style. A kiss on each cheek between men and between men and women is salutation French-style; the

Russian greeting entails at least three kisses. The hand-shake, bear hug, and other forms of physical entanglement represent different measures of feeling that seek expression in a greeting. The use of secret code words in greeting or a salutation by means of hand or finger gestures is for imaginative children or for the members of childishly adult organizations who refuse to abandon the mysterious symbols of their youth. The purpose of a greeting is to express joy; if there is none, express none.

Self-Expression

We must know ourselves. If this will not help us to discover truth, at least it will serve as a rule of life, and there is nothing better.

Blaise Pascal

Nobody can give you freedom. Nobody can give you equality or justice or anything. If you're a man, you take it.

Malcolm X, 1965

Give me six lines written by the most honest man in the world, and I shall find enough evidence in them to hang him.

Cardinal Richelieu, 1625

All life, all creation is tell-tale and betraying. A man reveals himself in every glance and step and movement and rest.

Ralph Waldo Emerson, 1877

You cannot help but express yourself: the problem is that of achieving a balance between such self-restraint that may lead to a vanishing act and such lack of restraint tantamount to unleashing a flood. Spontaneity is delightfully civil and can only be achieved through exercise of restraint having the appearance of effortlessness.

Sex

The cock swan is an emblem or representation of an affectionate and true husband to his wife above all other fowls; for the cock swan holdeth himself to one female only, and for this cause

nature hath conferred on him a gift beyond all
others: that is, to die joyfully, that he sings
sweetly when he dies.

Lord Coke, 1592

It is right to pursue advantage with moderation;
too sharp is the sting of madness arising from
unattainable aspirations.

Pindar

Men have unrealized potential for self-culti-
vation, self-direction, self-understanding, and
creativity. It is this potential that we regard as
crucial and to which we appeal, not to human
potentiality for violence, unreason, and submission to authority. The goal of man and society
should be human independence: a concern not
with the image of popularity but with finding a
meaning in life that is personally authentic;
a quality of mind not compulsively driven by a
sense of powerlessness, nor one which unthink-
ingly adopts status, values, nor one which re-
presses all threats to its habits, but one which
has full, spontaneous access to present and
past experiences . . . an active sense of curiosity, an ability and willingness to learn.

S.D.S. Port Huron Statement, 1962

The human race can survive through sexual
activity alone, but sexual activity alone cannot sustain
the human race. Activity—mental, physical, spiritual,
cultural—toward others, with others, and away from
others are sustaining activities. Sex, when the creation of
new life is the objective, is outside the realm of civility.
But sex as an expression of life, as an advantage to be
possessed even fleetingly, is inseparable from other life-
sustaining activities. It is an act not toward or away
from—but *with*—another, and it gains in civility as it

gains in candid recognition of what each mutually agrees
to share of himself with the other. Sex lacking in
candor lacks civility. Sex should observe these rules:

1. No secrecy. Furtive sex is akin to espionage,
betrayal, and other warlike destructive activity.
2. No self-deception. Fantasy is akin to decep-
tive advertising and other fraudulent business
practices.
3. No exploitation. Using another human being
for personal advantage is shoddy and cruel: sex
is not an act of political expression or a course
of education; neither is it a ritual or therapy.
Sex prompted by a need for consolation, reward, punishment, or anger is an abuse.
4. No regrets.

Smoking

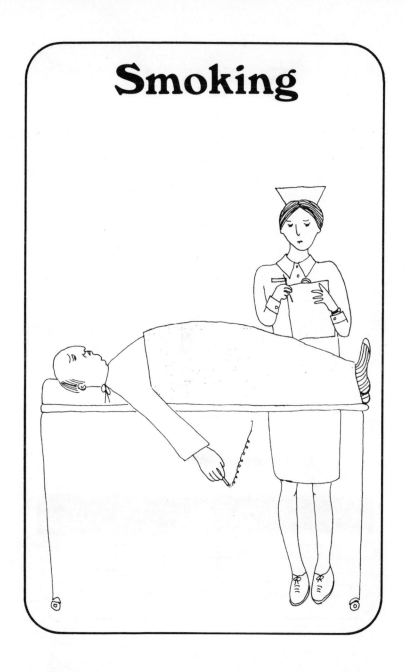

Warning: The Surgeon General Has Determined
That Cigarette Smoking Is Dangerous to Your Health.

Solitude

The eternal silence of those infinite spaces strikes me with terror.

Blaise Pascal

Solitude gives birth to the original in us, to beauty unfamiliar and perilous—to poetry. But also, it gives birth to the opposite: to the perverse, the illicit, the absurd.

Thomas Mann, 1912

What about man, this strange and pathetic individual, who is so insignificant in the coherences and incoherences of nature and of history and so significant to himself and to the people who love him? . . . What are you going to do with the pathos of individual existence? And what are you going to answer when he asks the question, "What is the meaning of my individual and my collective destiny, anyway?"

Reinhold Niebuhr

Civility can lead to the sense of having been emptied out, depleted. So much giving, and there is no end in sight, nor should there be. Fortitude and forbearance are motley makeup, shadows. The riches of the mind and feeling are the springs of their own renewal. Such nurturing is called solitude.

Sports

Games played with the ball, and others of that nature, are too violent for the body and stamp no character on the mind.

Thomas Jefferson

Work consists of whatever a body is obliged to do. . . . Play consists of whatever a body is not obliged to do.

Mark Twain

Any man who has to ask about the annual up-
keep of a yacht can't afford one.

J. P. Morgan

In sport, in courage, and the sight of Heaven,
all men meet on equal terms.

Winston Churchill

A spectator of sporting events takes part in
entertainment and not in sport. The same may be said
of gambling: he who gambles is concerned with the
outcome of the event rather than participation in it.
Most sporting events that rely on large numbers of spec-
tators are mainly concerned with making money—
legally and illegally—and civilization would suffer no
great loss if they were to disappear. Rugged sports that
depend on intense, fierce competition between two indi-
viduals or teams are generally hazardous even with, and
especially without, the benefit of expensive protective
equipment. Regular, moderate exercise, like walking,
swimming, bicycling, that can be done alone or with
companions is all that is needed for health and a sense
of fitness. Sports, games, or other recreations that re-
quire two or more people, including team competitions,
should be pursued if they provide a means for cheerful-
ness, learning, and an exchange of thought.

Tips

There is only an illusory difference between tipping a doorman and giving a Christmas gift to the mailman. There is very little difference between tipping a taxicab driver or a bellhop and bribing a judge or a congressman. How much an employee receives from his employers for his services should be determined by contract between the two of them and should in no way depend on the generosity, miserliness, or embarrassment of a client, customer, patron, or whatever other term is used. The quality of services performed should not be based on the anticipation of a special reward. Good services are being purchased by the customer and no surtax should be imposed in the form of a tip. The time to end this vestige of medieval gratuitousness is now!

Toasts

It is entirely fitting on any occasion where two or more people are gathered to offer something to drink— anything from tomato juice to champagne—and to raise glasses in a toast. The sole purpose of toasting is to create still another instance for the celebration of life. Simple one-word toasts do it, like "Cheers," "Health," "*Salut*," "Prosit." More involved sayings, or even short speeches, do it as well. What is to be avoided are the insincere formulas and sentiments. If there are not too many people involved, and if the glasses are not too fragile, there is an extra element of joy in clinking.

Travel

Only fools want to travel all the time; sensible men want to arrive.

Metternich

As the Spanish proverb says, "He who would bring home the wealth of the Indies must carry the wealth of the Indies with him." So it is in traveling: a man must carry knowledge with him, if he would bring knowledge home.

Samuel Johnson

Travel is the shaper of youth.

Jean Jacques Rousseau

Get moving! The sweet confections of the herdsmen served in the tents of the Mongolian hills are sweeter in retrospect; the war-torn ruins of once splendid Phoenician and Grecian civilizations show more direction than origin. The cooperative cities springing up in the midst of the cornfields of Yugoslavia; the feverish hewing of roads in the jungles of the Matto Grosso; the silent acquiescence of citizens living under the iron fist of military dictators; the brooding aurora borealis of the North; the immense and oppressive tranquility of rain forests, snowdrifts, canyon, and ocean are not just sights and sounds to be ogled but the very fibers of life to be incorporated into the vital flesh of human experience. Get moving!

Urbanity

A man who deserves the name of a gentleman
will be careful in his conversation not to offend
a chaste ear.

Samuel Richardson

By all means be urbane. One side of it requires
a merriness of language that will turn ordinary meanings
around to surprise and delight but never give offense. The
other side involves a total avoidance of everything in
speech, manner, or gesture that is incongruous and
coarse.

Virtue

If ours the faults, the virtues too are ours.

Royall Tyler, 1787

The highest virtue is always against the law.

Ralph Waldo Emerson

Wisdom is knowing what to do next; virtue is doing it.

David Starr Johnson

We keep on deceiving ourselves in regard to our faults, until we at last come to look upon them as virtues.

Heinrich Heine

You are a man, not God; you are a human, not an angel. How can you expect to remain always in a constant state of virtue, when this was not possible even for an angel of Heaven, nor for the first man in the Garden?

Thomas a Kempis

In uncertain times, like the present, there are three virtues to be pursued with ardor:

• Seek out, unravel, comprehend, grasp, and accept your heritage as a set of facts and not as bondage or endowment; the actions and sentiments of ancestors—good and bad—do not pass gentically from one generation to the next.

• Be optimistic about the future; shape it, make it, as far as it is in your power to do so: the future simply does not *just* happen.

• Forgive errors but take appropriate steps to prevent their repetition.

Who Pays

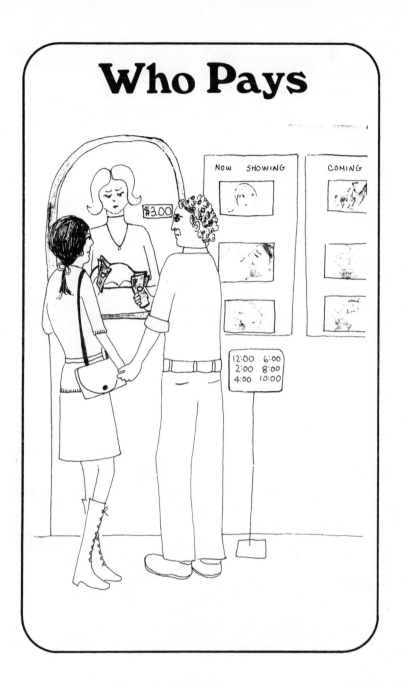

If you invite—pay!

If the occasion is not an invitation and there is something to be paid for, then make very explicit, frank arrangements by offering to pay, offering to share, or by being paid for.

Work

To crush, to annihilate a man utterly, to inflict on him the most terrible of punishments so that the most ferocious murderer would shudder at it and dread it beforehand, one need only give him work of an absolutely useless and irrational character.

Dostoevski, 1862

The wise man is cured of ambition by ambition.

La Bruyère

So great will be the frenzy of ambition that you will see nobody behind you if there is anyone in front of you.

Seneca, A.D. 64

Every man shall receive his own reward according to his own labor.

1 Corinthians

To labor is the lot of man below;
And when Jove gave us life, he gave us woe.

Homer

A man who gets his board and lodging on this ball in an ignominious way is inevitably an ignominious man.

H. L. Mencken

Soon—not soon enough, but soon—a guaranteed annual wage will permit people to choose the kind of work they genuinely want to do and that they are best equipped to do—or not to work at all. Most people work at unpleasant chores that they can't put their hearts into, and for a period of time each day that is more bound by convention than by principles governing the most efficient use of human labor. Soon people will be able to harness their interests and creative energies to the activities they believe in; the unpleasant tasks that cannot be performed by machines will be shared, each one assuming a portion of the burden.

Work only enough to satisfy your needs.

The text of this book was set on the linotype in Primer
by Maryland Linotype Composition Company.
The display face is Windsor.
The book was printed and bound at
Halliday Lithograph Corporation.
Designed by Jacqueline Schuman.